LIFE'S LEADERSHIP LESSONS

Lesli C. Myers

Life's Leadership Lessons

Copyright © Lesli C. Myers 2018

First Edition

Cover Design: Damian Brown

Front Cover Photo: Kareem Hayes,
Kareemhayesphotography.com

Back Cover Photo: ©Amy Moore Photography
amymoorephotography.com
@amymoorephoto

Editing: Wandah Gibbs, Ed. D.

ISBN-13: 978-1983780301
ISBN-10: 1983780308

WGW Publishing Inc, Rochester, NY

In Memory of,

My maternal grandmother, Mrs. Addie Terry Mills.
She taught me the power of leadership through life's
lessons.

Forward by Mr. Garth Fagan

Hair salons and barbershops have historically played a vital role in African-American communities. They provide an environment to talk about current events, politics, educational issues, social injustices, and the like. It's a haven where, pardon my pun, we literally and figuratively let our hair down. It is in this milieu that I first met Dr. Lesli C. Myers and had several deep and stimulating conversations surrounding a myriad of topics.

As a leader at the local, regional, national, and international levels, I've made it a point to follow the career of other leaders and have been particularly impressed by Lesli Myers' trajectory. I've watched her evolve over the past several years, and followed her rise to superintendent. Through the years we've also crossed paths at various formal functions and events and we share a large amount of respect for each other's accomplishments

Aside from her tremendous academic and professional pedigree, I'm impressed by the way she emanates both strength and approachability. She has a great sense of humor and on more than one occasion I've witnessed her veritable interest in people and what they have to say.

Through our conversations, especially those about my father and mother, I soon realized how much she values God, family, friends, colleagues, and especially the students she is responsible for serving. She knows how to have fun but her wheels are always turning as she seeks ways of improving educational opportunities for all. I love hearing the stories her Nana told and of the no nonsense advice provided by her mother and others.

The many mentors, guides, professors, family, and friends' lessons are captured and freely shared in this book. It takes courage to be so transparent and it requires a certain generosity to freely share what she has learned along the way. *Life's Leadership Lessons* is a compilation of Lesli Myers' reflections and lessons learned and is sure to inspire and challenge you as it has me. I for one will be keeping a copy on my desk!

GARTH FAGAN has been called "a true original," "a genuine leader," and "one of the great reformers of modern dance." "Originality has always been Mr. Fagan's strong suit, not least in his transformation of recognizable idioms into a dance language that looks not only fresh but even idiosyncratic."
-Anna Kisselgoff, The New York Times

Fagan is Founder and Artistic Director of the award-winning and internationally acclaimed Garth Fagan Dance, now celebrating its 47th season. The company's distinctive movement quality comes from years of training in Fagan Technique, the teaching method

Fagan developed hand in hand with his own dance vocabulary.

He has been recognized by a host of awards and honors including: Dance Magazine Award for "significant contributions to dance during a distinguished career," Golden Plate Award and induction into the American Academy of Achievement, Samuel H. Scripps American Dance Festival Award, "Bessie" (New York Dance and Performance) Award for Sustained Achievement, George Eastman Medal, Fulbright 50th Anniversary Distinguished Fellow, a Guggenheim Fellowship and honorary doctorates from the Juilliard School, the University of Rochester, Nazareth College, and Hobart and William Smith Colleges. Garth Fagan was selected as an "Irreplaceable Dance Treasure" by the Dance Heritage Coalition.

Mr. Fagan, a native of Jamaica, has been presented with that country's Order of Distinction in the rank of Commander, its Special Gold Musgrave Medal, for his "Contribution to the World of Dance and Dance Theater" and the Prime Minister's Award acknowledging his achievements.

A Distinguished Professor Emeritus of the State University of New York at Brockport. For his choreography of Walt Disney's, The Lion King, Fagan was awarded the Tony ® award, England's Laurence Olivier award, The Drama Desk, Outer Critics Circle, Astaire, Ovation, and Australia's Helpmann awards among other honors.

Table of Contents

Introduction

Over the River and Through the Woods is a Thanksgiving Day song by Ms. Lydia Maria Child. Originally a poem, it appeared in her *Flowers for Children*, volume 2, in 1844. It describes her childhood memories of visiting her grandparent's home.

I, too have fond childhood memories. My grandmother, the late Mrs. Addie Terry Mills (aka Nana) was a woman of distinction, faith, and zeal. She stood 5'10" with piercing hazel eyes that didn't miss a thing. What I admired most about my Nana was her ability to tell a story like none other.

During the holiday season, my friends would complain about perfunctory visits to their grandparents. I, on the other hand, was completely thrilled to see my grandmother and waited in excitement and expectation for one of her stories each time I went to visit. As soon as I entered my Nana's house she'd hug and kiss me, ask about my grades in school, make sure I was minding my parents, give me a piece of orange candy, then sit me down for my fill of wonderfully creative stories.

My grandmother's approach to storytelling was magical and entertaining. Each story, no matter how many times she told it, was filled with adventure, excitement, suspense, and always a *lesson learned*.

It is in that same spirit that I share these leadership lessons. Drawing on experiences from both my personal and professional life, I peel back varied aspects of my journey with the expectation that it provides each of you with inspiration, encouragement, and hope.

The book is divided into 31 short lessons, one for each day of the month. You'll notice that each one ends with the word, *Selah*, a Hebrew word used in the bible, particularly in the book of Psalms. It is believed that Selah signifies a musical interlude and suggests a time to pause and think about what was just said or sung; or a time to pause and watch for a visual demonstration of what was said or sung. You will have the opportunity to reflect upon and react to what you've read, then outline possible next steps.

From my leadership journey to yours.

Selah...

Dr. L

LCM Leadership Lesson #1
Your word is your bond.

We use words to communicate. Our expectations, emotions, and perspectives are demonstrated to others through our words. On average, we speak about 10,000 words per day. We freely use words but are we always cognizant of what we are saying and do we really mean what we say?

Being a person of our word is not always easy. We make verbal commitments in both our personal and professional lives, and though well intended, life happens and we become consumed with daily tasks.

I promised a colleague I would make cookies for a benefit she had become actively involved in to honor a friend she'd recently lost to cancer. She didn't ask me to make the cookies, I volunteered. I ended up working late the night before they were due and did not get in until close to bedtime. I thought about texting her and saying, "I'm just too tired. Sorry." And then I remembered what I'd promised.

You see, not only was she relying on me but this benefit was occurring to create a cheerful area for chemotherapy patients. A place where they could listen to music, watch movies, and play video games during treatments. I volunteered to make the cookies because my dad had lost his battle to cancer after many long days in the chemotherapy room. If I reneged on my promise, what would that have communicated to my colleague? So, with what little strength I had left that evening, I made 200 cookies from scratch before heading off to bed. My colleague was absolutely thrilled when I dropped the cookies off the next day.

A week later, I received a beautiful note thanking me for my delicious cookies along with pictures of the event.

What if I had decided not to make the cookies? I could have easily backed out or purchased some from a local bakery.

So, what's the leadership lesson here? Leaders keep their word and ensure they follow through on their commitments. Be mindful of the promises you make as you may never know just how impactful and meaningful your actions are to others.

Therefore, I ask a simple question, are you mindful of and purposeful about the promises you make?

Selah...

Dr. L

Personal Reflection/Action Items

_____

_____

_____

_____

_____

_____

_____

_____

LCM Leadership Lesson #2
I always feel like somebody's watching me.

It is said that true character is revealed when no one is watching, but I say that character is also revealed when EVERYONE is watching.

Have you ever noticed leaders who like to grandstand and who have a constant need to be in the limelight? They like to be seen by the *right* people and are all about talking to, and only interacting with *important people*. They also tend to be incredibly demanding and won't settle for anything they consider to be *beneath* them.

One evening I was at dinner with a group of coworkers. We were in the process of ordering from the menu when a colleague arrived late. He was incredibly demanding and rude to the waitress. She became visibly nervous and began to fumble the order, the silverware, and the dishes. He yelled at her about her incompetence and she fell apart.

Sensing her dismay, I pulled her to the side and apologized for his unacceptable behavior. I also told her that I thought she was doing a great job and I thanked her for her excellent service. Her confidence shifted and she made it through the evening.

Unfortunately, some leaders believe it is perfectly OK to act haughty, pretentious, and extremely demanding. This archaic style of leadership leaves no room for important characteristics such as being kind, gracious, patient, and humble in the presence of others? After all, people learn a lot about who you are by your actions and words.

I strive to remain unpretentious and free from behaviors and circumstances that might force me in to humility.

Leaders....I ask you today; are you mindful of how you behave when others are watching?

Selah...

Dr. L

Personal *Reflection / Action Items*

_____
_____
_____
_____
_____
_____
_____
_____
_____
_____
_____
_____
_____
_____
_____
_____
_____

LCM Leadership Lesson #3
Undercover boss.

Some leaders serve their organization and constituents from a balcony view. But I believe it is important to have a perspective on the entire organization and from a variety of angles. I also think it's important for us to see our organization at eye level and be on the dance floor with our people.

What does that look like? Have you ever seen the show, *Undercover Boss*? In this reality TV show, the chief executive officer changes his or her appearance and works with entry level employees to get a sense of whether operating procedures, interactions, and routines, are being followed as they should be. In the process, this CEO gets to know one or two workers extremely well by forming relationships with them. After some time, the boss reveals herself to the employees and shares the *lessons learned*.

I firmly believe that leaders shouldn't have to go *undercover* to learn more about the people in their employ, but when's the last time you spent quality time with people from all facets of your organization? Do you make time to come in early to set up or stay late to help clean up after an event? It's important to make meaningful connections and truly *be* with people.

I remember working late one evening and running into one of our custodians, who happened to be a new mom. On several occasions, she'd proudly shown me pictures of her little girl. I had found out earlier in the day however, that she had recently and unexpectedly lost her brother. I walked over to her and shared my condolences. She began to weep and I wrapped my arms around her. She went limp in my arms and sobbed. At that moment in time we were simply two individuals connecting at a very basic human level.

How does *Undercover Boss* translate into my work? I enjoy meeting with first year staff, walking the halls with security guards, riding the bus with the drivers, and spending time with children in the classroom. These actions help provide perspective into what's really going on in the organization. It also enables others to get to know me, my beliefs, and my heart. I can't tell you how many times someone has said to me, "You are not at all what I expected you to be!" I simply smile to myself and go on with my work.

So, I ask you leaders, "When's the last time you got out on the dance floor?"

Selah...

Dr. L

Personal Reflection/Action Items

_____
_____
_____
_____
_____
_____
_____

LCM Leadership Lesson #4
Losing sight of the shore experiences.

"On ne découvre pas de terre nouvelle sans consentir à perdre de vue, d'abord et longtemps, tout rivage." One does not discover new lands without consenting to lose sight, for a very long time, of the shore. This is my favorite quote which is attributed to André Paul Guillaume Gide, a French author and winner of the 1947 Nobel Prize in Literature.

How many times have we tried to push others to challenge themselves or asked someone to do something completely outside of their comfort zone? There is nothing wrong with this expectation with one caveat: we must be willing to do the same.

Ten months into my new role, I proposed a daring course of action. This plan was the culmination of many months spent examining structures already in place and meant to address organizational needs. A wide variety of information both quantitative and qualitative was collected and reviewed.

During those ten months, I made sure I maintained a visible presence. My travels throughout the community revealed that additional supports were needed to ensure maximization of potential. The proposal presented to the board was an intentional effort to provide that support.

Though the plan was well thought out, purposeful, and made sense, it upset some stakeholders. "Who is this new leader making all these major changes while

abandoning our current traditions and values?"
Leaders must at times make drastic organizational
decisions, that are distinctive in their novelty and
which follow unchartered territory.

From time to time, my style of leadership involves
trekking down a path with no footsteps. It is there that
I discover I can actually overturn existing challenges,
obstacles, and barriers. How does this translate into
practice? I often find myself in situations that stretch
me and allow me to move from the static to the
dynamic.

So, I ask you, "What is your *losing sight of the shore*
experience?"

Selah...

Dr. L

Personal Reflection/Action Items

_____

_____

_____

_____

_____

_____

_____

_____

_____

_____

_____

_____

LCM Leadership Lesson #5
Leadership outliers.

In statistics, an outlier is a value that lies outside most of the other numbers in a set of data. That figure is unique and stands alone. So, you've probably heard the phrase, *it's lonely at the top.* I'd like to offer an alternative take on that popular saying (which almost always has a negative connotation).

Leadership should lead us outside of the norm and customary. Leaders innovate, create, dream, and not only think outside the box, they sometimes blow it up altogether as they reimagine situations. We might envision a concept that others frown upon. and they may even think it's crazy, claim that it's never been done before, or think that it will never work. Many people won't dare enter that space. It's uncomfortable, requires hard work, and defies logic. It's outlier territory.

Here's an outlier example. In early January we were preparing for a particularly busy budget season. We needed to trim a significant amount of money from the overall budget while continuing to offer quality programs and services for students and staff. My colleague and I met off campus and began brainstorming. We listed every idea that came to mind including the far-fetched and outlandish. We spent several minutes doing this then began to narrow down our ideas. We finally decided upon a course of action and supported it with research and best practices. The board and community approved it months later, however, there were others who both openly and secretly shunned our decision believing it would fail. Not only did the program prove to be extremely successful, it served our most vulnerable students and is still in existence today.

Here's the cool part, leaders take an outlier to the next level by **making something happen.** While others may label it as a crazy and unlikely concept, it's really a living, breathing, and working outlier. Leaders not only survive there, they thrive in this space. I know I do! Some of the best things happen in outlier territory.

So, as you continue your quest to leave your imprint on the world, ponder the following question; what are the outliers on your personal and professional scatter plot and how do you plan to actualize them?

Selah...

Dr. L

Personal Reflection / Action Items

_____

_____

_____

_____

_____

_____

_____

_____

_____

_____

LCM Leadership Lesson #6
And now, here's the rest of the story.

I was working as a central office administrator and had a veteran administrator as my supervisor. I enjoy working in a fast-paced environment with significant challenges and this community was no exception. Parents had extremely high expectations, there was a competitive college nearby, and student issues were constantly brewing. We felt as though we spent an inordinate amount of time putting out wildfires.

I learned much while working with this administrator. She was tough as nails and led with fierceness. I greatly admired her decision-making abilities and her strength in sticking with the consequences of those decisions. Nonetheless, over time, a situation arose that caused me to question her leadership.

We were dealing with a sensitive litigious student issue and had been advised by attorneys that there should be no contact with the family. My boss stayed the course with that advice even though community pressure was mounting for her to make a public apology of some sort. Although I didn't say anything to her about this, due to the seriousness of the infraction the student had suffered, I thought we needed to do *something*.

One day, I was unexpectedly called down to her office and asked to clear a space on my calendar because she had called a meeting with the student's family. During the meeting, there were no attorneys and no media in the room, just me, my boss, a parent, and the parent's friend. The tension in the office was palpable until my boss reached for the parent's hands and said the following: "I am a mother and a grandmother and I can only imagine the pain and turmoil you've been through during this horrible experience. I want to personally apologize for what happened." I watched as my boss choked up while continuing to deliver the most heartfelt apology. After a brief exchange they hugged, then the parent and her friend left the office.

The administrator remained quiet about this meeting, though she continued to take flak from community members. When I asked her why she didn't say anything in her own defense, she told me that apologizing was just the right thing to do and that was all that mattered. And now YOU know the *rest of the story.*

So, I ask you, what situations might have occurred in your personal or professional life that had an outcome few are aware of? What is your *right thing to do* experience?

Selah...

Dr. L

Personal Reflection/Action Items

LCM Leadership Lesson #7
The little lies they told me.

I was three and a half years old and I was bored. I had just come home from a swimming lesson and wasn't ready to settle down. My mom told me to play a little longer under the carport so I began skipping around. Suddenly, I lost my balance and fell head first towards the front door. I put my tiny hands in front of me to try and break the fall and my right arm went right through the storm door. Glass shattered all over as I fell to the floor. I was badly hurt as a large part of my arm had been cut all the way through.

I was rushed to the hospital and the process of putting me back together commenced. As the doctor prepared to sew me up, she told me that it wouldn't hurt. My mother quickly interjected and said that it would in fact hurt but that it was necessary so I could begin to heal. I sat there and watched while the doctor administered 36 stitches across my little arm. I cried out periodically, but made it through.

What's the leadership application here? Sometimes we tell *little lies* to make people feel better. We don't want to hurt their feelings. While in fact, a little lie can end up hurting more than telling the truth would have. Feedback is an important part of the growth process. It helps us identify characteristics that need polishing, which then allows us to turn areas of growth into strengths.

What little lies have we told others and how might we begin to foster growth by telling the truth in a constructive manner?

Selah...

Dr. L

Personal Reflection/Action Items

_____
_____
_____
_____
_____
_____
_____
_____
_____
_____
_____
_____
_____
_____
_____
_____
_____
_____
_____
_____
_____
_____
_____
_____

LCM Leadership Lesson #8
That still, small voice.

Advice is defined as guidance or recommendations concerning prudent future action, typically given by someone regarded as knowledgeable or authoritative. Synonyms include: guidance · counseling · counsel · help · direction · information · recommendations · guidelines · suggestions · hints · tips · pointers · ideas · opinions · views · input · words of wisdom. These are all positive and supportive words.

I entered the presidency of a nonprofit state association with warranted trepidation. There were downstate/upstate tensions, dwindling memberships, and a lack of cohesion between the members of the executive board. Although a seasoned educational leader, I was inexperienced in state association leadership so it was with a considerable amount of reluctance that I took the helm.

Each year, the nonprofit held an annual conference which was a major source of funding for the organization. I sought advice from a variety of sources relative to conference logistics and planning: executive board members, past presidents, as well as other state presidents. I received so many pointers it made my head spin.

What course of action should I take? Who should be chosen as keynote speaker? How many workshops must we offer? What is the timeline for certain deadlines? To make matters worse, every suggestion made was touted as the best option. My thoughts eventually came to a screeching halt. There were far too many recommendations. I must admit that I almost quit the leadership position. As I processed and tried to make sense of everything, I decided I would just go ahead and establish a direction for the conference. I then worked with the conference committee to plan what would turn out to be the most highly attended conference yet.

I seek advice when I'm stuck or having difficulty with a challenging situation. Obviously, I bring my viewpoint to situations, yet realize that seeking wise counsel allows me to broaden my perspective. But what about that still, small voice also known as your intuition or gut? While it's valuable to obtain input from others, there are times when you need to rely on just three friends: me, myself, and I.

So, what's the leadership application here? Develop the ability to become your own expert and learn how to separate concrete information from noise.

So, I ask you this, what steps can you take to cultivate and develop that inner voice?

Selah...

Dr. L

Personal Reflection / Action Items

LCM Leadership Lesson #9
On being your best self.

I was probably the most miserable I'd ever been at
work. After a successful career, things had started to
change with new leadership. My work was not valued,
my responsibilities shifted, and the confidence in my
own abilities began to dwindle. I felt completely
devalued. It began to show on my face, in my behavior,
and my work. Simply put, I had an attitude, was
unhappy, and I let everyone know it!

After several weeks of letting my *natural* side show, I
had a change in attitude. I considered the fact that my
colleagues, and direct reports were all watching. What
was I saying by both word and deed? I was physically,
mentally, and emotionally detached from my job.

One morning, unable to sleep, I arose early and turned
on the TV to watch an episode of *Law and Order*, or so
I thought. That still, small voice within was urging me
to change the channel, so I did. I stopped on an
inspirational speaker whose very words were: "Are you
unhappy with your job?" I felt as though the show had
been produced specifically for me. As the presenter
spoke of ways to overcome that challenge, I began to
further evaluate my recent behavior.

I knew right then and there that I needed to make a
change. I started that same day by reestablishing my
presence at work. How did I do that? I went back to
coming in early and leaving late. I put my heart and
soul into everything I did and I worked harder than

ever. My victory would come as I restored my reputation as a dedicated team player.

Are you unhappy with your current situation? Are you not in the job of your dreams? You, and only YOU have the power to change that. Stop complaining about your boss, the job, the conditions, and focus instead on being *your best self* regardless of the circumstances.

So, ask yourself, what have I been cantankerous about and how can I effectively make the necessary emotional and behavioral shifts that will exemplify the best possible me?

Selah...

Dr. L

Personal Reflection/Action Items

_____

_____

_____

_____

_____

_____

_____

_____

_____

_____

_____

_____

_____

LCM Leadership Lesson #10
If you do it during practice, you'll do it in the game.

My varsity basketball coach used to say that in practice each time we'd try to cut corners, complain about a drill, or slack off. Whenever he'd call us on our behavior, we'd roll our eyes then go and re-do the drill.

Practice is not exciting. It's monotonous, unglamorous, and there's no audience. "Why in the world do we have to do this over, and over again? I get it already, and I know what to do in an actual game!"

Practice develops a skill base. Practice allows us to physically and mentally prepare to perform in a wide range of situations. Practice helps us build confidence, strength, and durability. Practice transforms incompetence into competence and helps conscious actions move to the unconscious.

How does this translate to leadership? No one starts at the top of the ladder or game. We work our way to the proverbial top, and to get there, it takes dedication, persistence, sweat, determination, and lots of practice. If you cut corners, come in late, leave early, and don't dedicate yourself to excellence along the way, you will never make it to the starting line-up.

So, I say to you THIS day, how's your practice going?

Selah...

Dr. L

Personal Reflection / Action Items

LCM Leadership Lesson #11
I need help!

The dictionary defines help as an appeal for urgent assistance; Making it easier for (someone) to do something by offering one's services or resources.

Great leaders frequently offer their assistance to colleagues and subordinates. We brainstorm, offer feedback, and help problem-solve. However, leaders are often reluctant to ask for help themselves. Perhaps we believe it demonstrates weakness or shows a chink in our armor. On the contrary, it illustrates we are human, are team players, and most importantly, it shows we need and recognize the skills, talents, and abilities of others.

My **executive assistant** is a phenomenal teammate. She has good instincts and often forecasts my needs before I identify them. Late one afternoon, I was working on an important project for which I had underestimated the time needed for completion. I was close to tears when she walked into my office. "Are you ok?" She asked. I paused before responding because I didn't want to appear incompetent or inept. "Deb, I did not realize this was going to take such a significant amount of time to complete. I'm going to be up all night finishing this project. Is there any way you can help me with this?" Without hesitation, she agreed to do so. She first went home to feed her family then came right back to help. We plugged away and together we completed everything on time.

Pride, embarrassment, ego, self-centeredness, and other emotions may block our ability to ask for help. Here's the irony, although we will eventually resolve most issues, we limit ourselves to endless possibilities and options. In as much as an addict must first acknowledge he has a problem, we must learn to express our need for assistance. So here goes: "My name is Lesli Clara Myers and I need your help!" See, it's that easy!

Take a moment to identify an area where you may need help and decide whom you might ask to assist you...

Selah...

Dr. L

Personal Reflection/Action Items

_____

_____

_____

_____

_____

_____

_____

_____

_____

_____

_____

_____

_____

_____

LCM Leadership Lesson #12
Practicing purposeful forgiveness.

I'm going to refer to scripture from the Holy Bible for this leadership lesson. In no way am I trying to blaspheme or rewrite text, but I'd like to look at some of the last words uttered by Jesus Christ as recorded in Luke 23:24. He said, "Forgive them for they know not what they do." I'd like to add that leaders need to also forgive those who KNOW *what they do.*

People are human, have weaknesses, and make mistakes, however, there are those individuals who purposefully develop schemes and plans meant to hurt, disrupt, embarrass or thwart. This perspective often comes from a place of insecurity or jealousy.

As leaders, we must learn to take the high road even though we may want to display righteous indignation. We need to forgive and do it quickly because resentment can settle in and ruin you. It is critical to learn how to forgive and move on. People will fail us again and again but we mustn't hold that against them.

You may be saying, "I hear you Dr. L. but have you ever had to forgive?" To that I respond with a resounding yes! I've had relatives, colleagues, community members, church folk, and friends hurt me deeply. I've been talked about, lied to, and schemed against.

But here's the saving grace, there is so much power in forgiveness. It can help transform deep hurt and anger into peace. Forgiveness can also help you overcome rejection, conflict, sadness, fear, and uncertainty. It is about making the conscious decision to let go of the resentment.

So, on this day, as said by our former First Lady Michelle Obama, "When they go low, we go high." Forgive today and each additional day that the related emotion resurfaces. Eventually you will be free.

So, consider any unforgiveness you are allowing to hold you captive and ask yourself, "What am I waiting for before letting go?" List the ways in which you will benefit by forgiving.

Selah...

Dr. L

Personal Reflection / Action Items

_____

_____

_____

_____

_____

_____

_____

_____

_____

_____

_____

_____

_____

LCM Leadership Lesson #13
Birds of a feather flock together.

If you are familiar with the social media application LinkedIn, you are probably aware of its *People Also Viewed* section. This feature allows you to see whose profile people have looked at before or after they've viewed yours. In other words, probably subscribers who have similar characteristics and interests to yours.

This leads me to the focus of this leadership lesson. Who exactly are you? What specific characteristics do you possess and are they noteworthy? And because of those characteristics, who are you drawing in to your inner circle?

Leaders must forever be willing to look inward and participate in reflective practice. Every so often I think about what makes me who I am. Are there any areas I need to work on? Am I fully maximizing the gifts, talents, and abilities with which I've been endowed?

I then reflect on those whom I call friend. The ones who are a part of my *crew*. Do these individuals sharpen my sword and in turn do I add value to them? Whether we like it or not, we are judged by the company we keep.

People often evaluate you based on the behaviors and actions of those closest to you. They may suppose that those who hang together have similar behaviors, and although you may be different from the company you keep, people who do not know you very well will make their own assumptions. Whether it's fair or not, you will be judged in relation to the people you associate with.

"Surround yourself with the dreamers and the doers, the believers and thinkers, but most all, surround yourself with those who see greatness within you, even when you don't see it yourself."

-Steve Jobs

So, I ask you not only to think about those you choose to spend time with but also to think about the value you add and how you might positively enrich others?

Selah...

Dr. L

Personal Reflection/Action Items

_____
_____
_____
_____
_____
_____
_____
_____
_____
_____
_____
_____

LCM Leadership Lesson #14
Do you have the right to remain silent?

This lesson revolves around a conversation between Clarice and Hannibal Lecter in the movie *Silence of the Lambs*. In exchange for help with her investigation, Lecter forces Clarice to tell him information about her personal life. She shares memories from her childhood which occurred after she'd been sent away to live with her uncle in West Virginia. He owned a sheep and horse farm, and she learned one night that the lambs on the farm were going to be slaughtered. In horror, she runs away. The implication in the movie is that Clarice will no longer be awakened by the screaming lambs in her dreams, the lambs she was unable to save. Instead, in her role as a government agent, she will save innocent victims because she will have ended her silence.

The late Reverend Dr. Martin Luther King Jr. is credited with saying, "A man dies when he refuses to stand up for that which is right. A man dies when he refuses to stand up for justice. A man dies when he refuses to take a stand for that which is true."

There is much going on in the world, in our nation, our state, our region, and our communities. Hatred, poverty, bigotry, violence, and hopelessness regularly fill the news and our social media timelines.

It is my opinion that we can no longer rest in the luxury of complacency. Now I'm a realist and I know I can't do everything, "but I can certainly do something and I refuse to let what I cannot do, interfere with what I can."   -Edward Everett Hale

So, I pose three simple questions for you to cogitate and hopefully act upon:

If not me...then who?
If not here...then where?
If not now...then when?   -Hillel the Elder

What are you currently keeping silent about?

Selah...

Dr. L

Personal Reflection/Action Items

LCM Leadership Lesson #15
Sous-chef de cuisine.

Wikipedia defines a sous-chef de cuisine (French for under-chef of the kitchen), as a chef who is second in command in a kitchen; the person ranking next after the executive chef. Generally, a good sous-chef will eventually receive a promotion to executive chef.

Meanwhile, the sous-chef is described as having many responsibilities. They oversee all kitchen tasks, train new chefs, and ensure customers always receive quality meals that are aesthetically pleasing. Additionally, a sous-chef must thoroughly understand how to use and troubleshoot all appliances and cooking instruments in the event of a malfunction. A sous-chef is required to discipline any kitchen staff who may have acted against restaurant policy. They also need to be responsive and resourceful when problems arise, and are responsible for ensuring that all safety and sanitary precautions are strictly adhered to in maintaining a safe work environment.

My close friends and colleagues know that I enjoy cooking and baking. I watch many television shows on the *Food Network* and work diligently at improving my cooking skills.

I recently had the chance to be sous-chef to my fiancé Randy. He was making his famous gumbo and I decided to help prep some of the ingredients. He was very specific when telling me how he wanted the onions and peppers cut and reminded me that all shells must be carefully removed from the shrimp. I got irritated for a moment because I thought, "I know how to cook well and I don't need someone to tell me how!"

And then it occurred to me that even though I am a leader in and outside of the kitchen, I can always learn something new. I don't know the varied nuances of making excellent gumbo whereas he does. I was reminded of the importance of welcoming direction and feedback. This valuable information can be used to help make decisions. Top performers welcome feedback as they search for ways to make their best even better.

What's the leadership application here? Leaders must be humble enough to realize they don't know everything. We have a certain set of skills but those colleagues around us (if we hired well), also have valuable skills. When was the last time you allowed someone else to run a meeting, make a major decision, or take the lead role, even for a moment? Are you ready and able to occasionally serve as sous-chef?

Selah...

Dr. L

Personal Reflection/Action Items

_____

_____

_____

_____

LCM Leadership Lesson #16
Problems are nothing but the flip side of an opportunity.

Though I'd been a high school counselor for just a few years, I knew that a major aspect of the job involved keeping track of credits each student accumulated towards graduation. I kept meticulous notes and my record keeping was impeccable...or so I thought. In early spring, I checked through all my seniors' records and noticed that one of the students was missing a credit to graduate. I calmly called her in to my office to ask her about the class. She immediately realized the gravity of the situation and began to cry. After assuring her we would fix this issue, I went into problem-solving mode.

I made an appointment with my administrative supervisor to inform him of the situation. A critical component my principal had taught me was that it was ok to make a mistake, but it was important to come forward with at least one solution towards resolving the issue.

When I met with him later that day, I presented the situation and before he could react, I shared five possible solutions that could help my student recoup the missing credit. I carefully outlined each course of action including the pros and cons and related outcomes. Each option provided a viable opportunity for my student to earn the needed credit. After reviewing each one carefully, we landed on a successful choice.

What's the leadership lesson here? It's easy to face difficulties from a deficit perspective. We may deem a situation hopeless with no prosperous ending in sight. However, if learn to face challenges as opportunities to develop solutions, the desired results become that much more attainable.

Ask yourself, "How can I position myself so when difficulties arise, I have viable options to address those challenges?" I also ask you to think about how you might effectively analyze situations and creatively develop multiple solutions.

Next time you face what seems to be an insurmountable challenge, flip the script and say "Houston, we have an opportunity!"

Selah...

Dr. L

Personal Reflection/Action Items

_____
_____
_____
_____
_____
_____
_____

LCM Leadership Lesson #17
Staying in your lane.

I spend a significant amount of time driving and it can be particularly daunting when I'm under pressure to get somewhere at a specific time. To reduce the time in transit, I sometimes weave in and out of traffic lanes to avoid someone who is driving too slowly. What I've discovered over time however is fascinating; the same car I passed and left behind me, often arrives near my destination at the same time I do. Here's the kicker: they stayed in their lane the entire time while I was busy bobbing and weaving all over the place.

Once, when I was facing a particularly challenging and complex personnel matter, it became imperative that I quickly assemble our leadership team. With minimal time to notify multiple stakeholders, organize press releases, formulize plans, and communicate with local and regional law enforcement, we sat down to devise a plan of action. Several department heads then coordinated efforts to deliver a well thought out plan.

Though there are times when a leader must act alone in setting a direction, in this complicated instance, each of us benefitted from our individual skillsets and contributed in the handling of multiple matters in perfect synergy. No one tried to take the lead and solve the issue outside their realm of expertise. Given the unique nature of the situation, what could have been a mismanaged and slipshod reaction to a crisis, resulted instead in a well-orchestrated response.

Staying in your lane is a popular saying that suggests the importance of minding your own matters, carrying your weight, and effectively managing your area of responsibility. People are depending on your ability to step up to the plate and produce. But if you are overly concerned with trying to play catcher, outfielder, pitcher, and second base, you could jeopardize your ability to effectively play on first base. Too often we try to be a Jack or Jill of all trades, rather than master of a few things.

We may not excel in all things, but as leaders, we must constantly sharpen our skills, ensuring we continue to be a productive, contributing member of the team.

As you reflect below, consider an area or two of growth that may need polishing? What might be required to turn any identified deficits into strengths?

Selah...

Dr. L

Personal Reflection / Action Items

_____
_____
_____
_____
_____
_____
_____
_____

LCM Leadership Lesson #18
Ubuntu: I am because we are.

When I was younger, I loved putting puzzles together. I approached the task by ripping open the box, dumping the pieces on the table, finding every piece with a straight edge, creating the frame, and completing the puzzle, periodically looking at the box for guidance. Once finished, I would gaze proudly at the 1,000-piece work of art I'd successfully completed.

By definition; inclusivity is the policy or procedure of not excluding members or participants on the grounds of defining factors such as gender, race, class, sexuality, disability, etc. So, you might ask, what do puzzle pieces have to do with inclusivity? What if I had decided to exclude a puzzle piece because I didn't like it, understand it, or feared the color, shape or size of that piece? I would not be able to complete the task at hand and the puzzle would be incomplete. Let me repeat...the puzzle would be incomplete.

I was only five years old when I came home one day from summer camp crying. While surrounded by a group of other campers, a girl had said to me, "You can't play with us because we are all vanilla ice cream cones and you are a chocolate ice cream cone." I felt crushed and humiliated particularly because everyone had started laughing. I rushed home to have a conversation with my mom. She sat me down and said, "Honey, when we go to the ice cream parlor, what kind of ice cream does Daddy get?" "Rum raisin," I replied.

"And what kind does Mommy like?" "Strawberry," I said. "And what is your favorite?" "Pistachio!" "Do you only find vanilla and chocolate at the ice cream store?" "No," I replied. "So, you see, sometimes you have a hard time picking just one flavor because there are so many to choose from. Just as ice cream comes in many flavors, so do people!" She then wiped my tears away and off I ran to play.

As Deepak Chopra is quoted saying, "There are no extra pieces in the universe. Everyone is here because he or she has a place to fill, and every piece fits into the greater puzzle." Inclusivity allows us to see multiple perspectives, challenge our current way of thinking, and provides us opportunities to expand our horizons.

Take a moment to pause and ponder how you might broaden your connections to others to potentially expand your world.

Selah...

Dr. L

Personal Reflection/Action Items

_____

_____

_____

_____

_____

_____

LCM Leadership Lesson #19
A letter to my younger self.

Dear Lesli,

One of our family's most difficult times occurred following the day Dad received news he had cancer. You started to crumble even though he took it like a champ. He responded to his new life sentence with one of his favorite sayings, "I'll deal with the hand I've been dealt." He then proceeded to enjoy his life to the fullest for several more years, even after receiving word that his cancer had returned.

Sometime later, you stood valiantly at your father's bedside. You spoke life into him, and thanked him for everything he'd done for you. You told him you loved him, and that you would continue to be brave in his absence.

After several hours of talking, praying, singing, and waiting; at 11:27pm on August 28, 2003 Dr. Earl T. Myers took one last deep breath and died. Respectfully, you closed his eyes as you touched his handsome face for the very last time. You were very brave.

Ironically, at the time of Dad's death, your career had begun to take off. You were already supervising several counselors and social workers, and managing a host of other responsibilities in one of the largest school districts in New York state. You were coordinating grief and trauma efforts relating to horrible situations involving students, community members, and staff. You consoled, hugged, counseled, and supported numerous individuals though you yourself were emotionally paralyzed.

And then it happened...You dropped to your knees a little over a month after his death. Tears streaming down your face you uttered repetitively, "I can't believe he's gone...my daddy's dead and never coming back!" Neither your younger sister nor your cousin could console you. They both stared at you in shock and disbelief. They were very worried because you had always been the strong one.

If I could go back to that time and place, I would lovingly get down in the middle of the kitchen floor with you and rock you until your tears subsided. I would gently tilt your face towards mine and firmly say to you: *counselor* you cannot heal thyself. Acknowledge your hurt and your pain so you can go and continue to make your indelible mark on this world.

What you don't yet realize is that you will continue to carry on your father's iconoclastic legacy. You will earn your doctorate, will testify before the United States Congress on behalf of school children, and successfully secure millions of dollars in educational funds. You will honor your father's legacy by becoming the first African-American female to be both president of the New York State School Counselor Association and a superintendent of schools in Monroe County.

-Lesli

Though leaders experience unbearable pain and walk through unexpected seasons in life, once we have spent the necessary time healing, we will discover the strength to go on.

Think of a moment along your life's journey where you became emotionally paralyzed. What steps did you take to get yourself back to participating in regular activities? How did you do it?

Selah...

Dr. L

Personal Reflection/Action Items

_____

_____

_____

_____

_____

_____

_____

_____

_____

_____

_____

_____

_____

_____

_____

_____

_____

LCM Leadership Lesson #20
All I see is a bunch of trees!

Autumn is my favorite time of year! Football is in full force and on the weekends, you often see youth and adults alike outside playing pickup games. The weather changes and the air becomes crisp and refreshing. This is when I put on my favorite sweater and pull the turtleneck up over my nose. The leaves are particularly vibrant with brilliant hues of orange, red and yellow. As a child, I so loved jumping in the leaves after school.

My mom, younger sister, and I were taking our annual fall trip to visit my maternal grandmother. Traveling from upstate New York to Atlantic City, New Jersey is very scenic in the fall. Mom and I were excitedly *oohing and ahhing* at the foliage and making comments about its beauty, vivacity, and magnificence. The conversation continued off and on throughout the trip.

A few hours into our trek, my sister let out a big sigh and I turned around to see her little arms tightly folded across her chest. I said, "Linda, what's the matter?" With the typical innocence of a seven-year-old she proclaimed, "You and Mom keep talking about foliage but all I see is a bunch of stupid trees that aren't even green anymore!"

What's the leadership lesson here? Each organization has a mission, vision, values, and goals statement, and a list of strategic priorities. Much time is put into ensuring those tenets are well-articulated. Unfortunately, unless extra care is spent on making sure everyone in the organization speaks the same language, oftentimes those in senior management are the only ones who know them by heart.

Although all three of us had the same view along that drive, only two of us were speaking the same language, while the third had no understanding of what we were talking about. It's important that leaders ensure they are using common language and that they embed checks for company-wide understanding along the way.

Is there anything you might need to circle back on to ensure there is common understanding throughout the entire organization?

Selah...

Dr. L

Personal Reflection / Action Items

_____
_____
_____
_____
_____
_____
_____
_____
_____
_____

LCM Leadership Lesson #21
The power of speaking things into existence.

I love formal learning. If I could go to school for the rest of my life, I would. I returned to college to obtain my second master's degree, this time in educational administration. The program was intensive and was designed to train teachers to become administrators. In addition to the classes on Friday nights and Saturday mornings, there was a significant amount of coursework and an associated internship.

Dr. Fran Murphy was one of the professors providing oversight for the program. He is brilliant and has a story for everything. In every one of his classes, I sat mesmerized as he regaled us with examples from his vast experience as a school leader in educational administration. Students were constantly vying for his attention.

One requirement of the program was to discuss our short and long-term plans. When I met with Dr. Murphy I was ready to disclose my plan. He asked me, "So Lesli, what is your ultimate administrative goal?" I told him I thought I'd like to end up in the district office overseeing school counselors, creating and delivering targeted professional development, and crafting equitable programs and services for students. He leaned in, looked me directly in the eye, and said, "You will end up doing that and then some, but you will never be fully satisfied in your career until you become a superintendent of schools!"

I sat in front of him, dumbfounded. There was no way I wanted to be a superintendent. It is a public position that requires significant sacrifice. I wasn't averse to working hard but I'd seen the physical and emotional toll the role of superintendent had taken on colleagues. I respectfully yet firmly told him that being a superintendent was not a viable option for me. He sat back in amusement and said, "Just wait and see." Our conversation and meeting ended on that note.

After graduating from the program my formal administrative journey began. I kept in touch with Dr. Murphy over the years and sought his council on difficult matters. His mentorship and support have been invaluable and I know he is always there should I need to seek him out. As leaders, we never outgrow the need for a solid mentor. Naturally when I became superintendent I called Dr. Murphy to let him know. I left a simple message and all I said was, "Dr. Murphy, it's Lesli. I'm calling to let you know that you were right."

Is there anything someone predicted for you that was immediately dismissed because it seemed too big? Ask yourself what you are afraid of, then decide to at least entertain the possibility.

Selah...

Dr. L
(Note: Opportunity for reflection following lesson #22)

LCM Leadership Lesson #22
Get gritty with it!

Anyone who's ever worked on their doctorate knows it's the most challenging academic journey you will ever embark upon. You learn research methodology and get familiar with the Institutional Review Board's process, while trying to determine how you might successfully contribute to an existing body of knowledge. And then, there's that *big paper* at the end: the dissertation.

I was at the tail end of that journey and just a few months away from defending my dissertation. All my coursework was complete, but in order to defend, I needed my dissertation to also be complete. I felt I was nowhere near this goal and tried to convince myself several times that it would be OK for me to remain, *All But the Dissertation* (ABD) status.

I had an extremely intense moment one Saturday afternoon while sitting in the school library. I thought about the significant amount of writing I still needed to do and I began to crumble emotionally. I looked over at my classmate Andrea and said, "I need to take a break, I'll be back." I left my coat and my phone at the table and just started walking and crying as I went through several buildings, travelled up and down hills, and meandered along streets throughout the campus. I remember eventually walking up to a tree, then leaning in to hug it while I sobbed. Yes, I said it right, I sobbed and hugged a tree. I'm sure students witnessing this display of emotion thought about calling campus security.

Have you ever cried so much that you literally run out of tears? Well that was me that day. I knew I had a decision to make. Was I going to quit or was I going to tough it out? I was seriously contemplating this as a myriad of thoughts were going through my mind. Suddenly, within that moment, I came to a definitive conclusion. My pedigree would not allow me to quit. My dad put himself through school (a bachelor's, two master's degrees, and a doctorate), and he had far less resources and support than I did. My grandmother's words (see lesson #31) rang through my mind. I had no valid excuse for quitting. So, I squared up my shoulders and headed back to the library where I got an earful from my friend Andrea.

She reaffirmed my decision when she said to me, "Girl, if earning a doctorate were easy more people would have *Dr.* in front of their name. We've both got this, and one day we will be Dr. Cain and Dr. Myers!" With that said we forged ahead and soon after, each of us successfully defended our dissertation. What's the leadership application here? Recognize that at times you will feel disheartened along your journey, but in the grand scheme of things, it's a short-lived experience. Acknowledge your feelings, then pick yourself up and keep moving forward! You can and will make it!

Describe a time where you needed to be *gritty*. Reflect on how you moved forward. Are you currently stuck? Think of steps you can take today in moving forward.

Selah...
Dr. L

Personal Reflection/Action Items

_____
_____
_____
_____
_____
_____
_____
_____
_____
_____
_____
_____
_____
_____
_____
_____
_____
_____
_____
_____
_____
_____
_____

LCM Leadership Lesson #23
The power of unintended consequences.

An educator always has that one student they'll never forget. Danielle is that one for me. I met her when she was a freshman assigned to my caseload. Danielle was an average student and could easily have been what I term an *under the radar, invisible student.* She was shy and unsure of herself. She had striking hazel eyes, though when people complimented her on them, she usually rebuffed them.

We quickly bonded and she often popped into my office during lunch or before and after school. Over the course of four years, I learned a lot about Danielle, her dreams, hopes, joys, concerns, fears, and challenges. Whenever the topic of college arose, she would clam up believing that college was not an option for her. Together we worked on building her an academic portfolio that could garner college acceptance. Danielle was successfully accepted into college and I couldn't have been prouder.

Many years have passed since her high school graduation yet we continue to stay in touch with one another. Ironically, we share the same May 15th birthday, so we always connect on that day. We also try to see the Fourth of July fireworks together each year.

Danielle sent me this unexpected message a few years ago:

Ms. Myers. I got a call from my son's teacher saying that he wanted to drop out of his honors classes. His father and I, were discussing this with him when his dad said, "Next year, when you go to high school we're hoping you'll meet at least one teacher who will change your whole perspective on school and push you to be better, simply because she believes in you."

I then smiled, turned to my son, and explained how you had been that one adult for me. His face lit up and he asked, "The same Ms. Myers you always talk about that we go see fireworks with on the Fourth of July?" He couldn't believe that after so much time had passed, the impact you had on me and respect you earned was still so strong.

I am not sure if this story will influence him in the long run, but it did get his attention. I just wanted you to know that even after 20 years you are still my inspiration and I love you dearly.

-Danielle

As I read the message, I wept. I was at work at the time and my assistant came into my office to see what was wrong. I told her about the letter and the perceived, ongoing impact I'd had on Danielle's life.

What I had merely considered my role and responsibility as a school counselor had meant far more to Danielle. As a leader, never underestimate the long-term impact you might have on just one person while simply *doing your job...*

How might you maximize your interactions with others so the impact is meaningful and purposeful?

Selah...

Dr. L

Personal Reflection / Action Items

_____

_____

_____

_____

_____

_____

_____

_____

_____

_____

_____

_____

_____

_____

_____

_____

_____

_____

_____

_____

_____

_____

LCM Leadership Lesson #24
Failing forward.

Getting accepted into graduate school was an interesting experience for me. I had the opportunity to apply to a program where tuition, room, and board were completely waived upon successful acceptance to said program. I carefully completed an application that would surely allow me to secure one of the spots...or so I thought.

The day my acceptance letter arrived I tore it open with much anticipation. To my dismay, a portion of the letter read as follows:

Dear Ms. Lesli C. Myers,

Thank you for your application to our program. Unfortunately, after careful review of your paperwork, we are unable to offer you admission. Should you have any questions, please don't hesitate to contact us.

Sincerely,
The Admissions Committee

What do you mean I didn't get into the program? How could this be? I submitted a quality application, had impeccable references, and was a viable candidate.

Turns out I had fooled myself into thinking that my *less than stellar* grades during the first two years of undergraduate school would not impact me. Although I made the dean's list during my junior and senior years, my overall grade point average was not strong enough to get into this program. I represented a gamble to the admissions committee.

Some individuals may have accepted this rejection letter as the final say, but I refused to do so, and was determined that this would not be the *final answer*. I, along with another classmate, made an appointment with the dean to plead our case.

We were eventually accepted into the program under the condition we would be responsible for paying room and board, while they waived the considerable tuition. I was extremely grateful for a second chance and vowed to remain academically strong. I ended up graduating with a final GPA of 3.8.

So, what's the leadership application here? Everyone experiences failure. Our egos get bruised and we may want to quickly remove our toys from the sandbox and go home. Great leaders understand that failure is a necessary and important component of the leadership journey. It helps to humble us and forces us to hold a mirror up to ourselves so we can identify our deficits.

So, I ask that the next time you experience an unsuccessful result, that you pause before throwing in the towel. Acknowledge how you may have contributed to the outcome and consider how you might ensure that history does not repeat itself.

Selah...

Dr. L

Personal Reflection/Action Items

_____
_____
_____
_____
_____
_____
_____
_____
_____
_____
_____
_____
_____
_____
_____
_____
_____
_____
_____
_____
_____
_____
_____
_____

LCM Leadership Lesson #25

One is the magic number.

So many times, I define my pride
Through somebody else's eyes
Then I looked inside and found my own stride,
I found the lasting love for me
If I'm searching for my spirituality
Passionately I must begin with me

There's just me...
One is the magic number

-Jill Scott from the Album, *Who is Jill Scott, Words and Sounds*, Vol 1

Whenever I'm in the board of education meeting room, I look over at the wall where the picture of each former superintendent of schools is prominently displayed. Each superintendent had their platform, their issues to deal with, and their triumphs. There exists a strong legacy of tradition and values which is what drew me to the community.

My picture won't get placed on the wall until after I leave my position. I laugh to myself when imagining that day. People will say: duck, duck, duck, duck, duck, and when they get to my picture...goose! I posted this sentiment on social media and a well-meaning friend quickly responded saying, "Lesli you're not a goose, you're an eagle! No one knows what you've been through and what it takes to be a superintendent, especially during an age of extreme accountability and high need of transparency. And to top it off, you are young, female, and black. It hasn't been easy but those who have been watching you, realize that you take the role extremely seriously and they see the outpouring of joy you have in serving the children in your district."

Though I value every piece of the puzzle and rely on an incredible team, there are times when I realize there are steps on my journey that I must walk on my own.

The need to connect with others is natural. Family, friends, colleagues, and other supporters are important, but sometimes you need to keep it as simple as possible and begin with yourself. Time alone to ponder and reflect is vital in discovering that *one is the magic number.*

How do you decide when you need time to be alone? What goes into that decision?

Selah...

Dr. L

Personal Reflection/Action Items

_____
_____
_____
_____
_____
_____
_____

LCM Leadership Lesson #26
There is no I in team.

I love playing softball! I started playing with a group of friends at a local recreation center when I was in fourth grade. My love of the sport grew from there. What I appreciate most about softball is that you need both a solid offense and defense to have a successful outcome. No one individual makes up the entire team. Instead, it requires at least 10 people all working together towards a common goal.

I played on the same team for more than twenty years. Although players came and went over time, a core of us remained. We lived and breathed softball and often found ourselves reminiscing about a game or planning our approach for an upcoming one. Even during the off season, we came together for social events and looked forward to the four-month-long baseball season. We had four back-to-back years in which we won the championship, and if I'm not mistaken, our record shows only one loss during that entire stretch.

What made our team so successful? We certainly had athletic prowess which helps, but primarily we made sure we approached each game as a team, capitalizing on each other's strengths. We also had incredible team chemistry. It got to a point where we didn't have to say much prior to setting up for a batter.

Good leaders know how to *play nice* in the sandbox. They regularly share their toys with others and don't get territorial when someone enters their space. Most importantly, they make time to get to know their teammates' strengths and potential for growth.

What additional steps can you take to develop leadership capacity and learn how to value each member on your team?

Selah...

Dr. L

Personal Reflection/Action Items

_____

_____

_____

_____

_____

_____

_____

_____

_____

_____

_____

_____

_____

_____

_____

_____

_____

_____

_____

LCM Leadership Lesson #27
Walking the work-life balance tightrope.

Leadership is not without its challenges and when you first start out it can be particularly daunting. We work extremely hard to climb the corporate ladder and do everything we can to ensure we stay at the top. Working long hours, connecting with internal and external stakeholders, developing strategic plans for the organization, collaborating with the board, and remaining innovative, are just a fraction of what is required in my line of work. Oftentimes in the process of staying ahead of the game, family suffers as we struggle to maintain an appropriate and reasonable work-life balance.

During my first year as superintendent of schools I worked an average of 12-14 hours a day to ensure I was connecting with community, maintaining my visibility, and making sure our district was on track academically. I rarely had a moment to take a break to eat.

Finally, a colleague and I made time to connect for lunch and just as we were heading out of the office my cell phone rang. I glanced down at it and noticed it was my mom. She had already called me several times that morning and I was tempted to ignore the call. I reluctantly answered the phone only to hear an unfamiliar male voice on the other end. "Is this Dr. Lesli Myers?" Then he said, "This is your mother's neighbor and I'm calling to let you know that her house is on fire!" I thanked him for calling and immediately jumped into the car and raced towards my mom.

The 25-minute drive to her house was excruciating and I know I broke several traffic laws along the way. When I arrived, Mom was walking around aimlessly with nothing but the clothes on her back, and clutching her infamous purse. She had lost absolutely everything in the fire, including our beloved chihuahua Tully. I could not believe this had happened to MY mom. I am so glad I did not ignore that phone call.

What's the leadership lesson here? Family is a large component of my work-life balance and I mustn't allow my career to constantly supersede spending quality time with my mom. She now has an incurable, degenerative disease and lives in an assisted-living residence. There, concerts and other important social activities occur regularly. It absolutely makes her day when I come in and enjoy an event with her.

Ask yourself what might be hindering you from effectively balancing and prioritizing family and other personal matters? What steps might you take to carve out some time?

Selah...

Dr. L

Personal Reflection/Action Items

LCM Leadership Lesson #28
What is possible for one, is possible for another.

Eleanor Roosevelt said, "Do one thing every day that scares you." This is certainly much easier to say than to practice. I try to live my life without fear and intentionally work to reduce those personal and professional preoccupations that figuratively go bump in the night (and day).

Nonetheless, May of 2012 is forever etched in my mind as I remember slowly pulling into an empty parking space at school district headquarters. You see, I had applied for the position of superintendent. I paused while parking my car realizing I was much more nervous than I should have been for an interview. I was very aware that no one who looked like me; African-American and female, had ever been a permanent superintendent in Monroe County and yet I had the nerve, the gall, and the audacity to try and be the first. Doubt, fear, and anxiety reverberated in my mind. I thought, I can't do this, it is impossible. I will *never* become the chief executive officer of a public school district.

I then paused to think about all those who had both knowingly and unknowingly forged a path before me: my parents Dr. Earl and Mrs. Clara Myers, my mentor and friend Dr. Arthur *Sam* Walton who served as superintendent and as a deputy commissioner of education for New York state, Fannie Jackson Coppin the first African-American female principal and superintendent, Mary Jane Patterson, a school teacher considered to be the first African-American woman to earn a bachelor's degree, and Dr. Edward Alexander Bouchet, the first African-American to earn a Ph.D., completing his dissertation in physics at Yale in 1876.

I promptly shook the mental cobwebs away. I deserved to be here...this was my *Kairos* moment. My education, skills, and abilities made me more than a viable candidate for superintendent. Then my breakthrough occurred. I heard a still small voice speak to me and it emphatically shook me back to reality, "Girl...either go hard or go home!" The rest of the story is proverbial history. Therefore, I unequivocally say to you, when contemplating opportunities, know that what is possible for one, is possible for another.

What might be holding you back? Is there something you've been fearful of doing that you might begin to tackle today?

Selah...

Dr. L

Personal Reflection/Action Items

_____

_____

_____

_____

_____

_____

LCM Leadership Lesson #29
Do what matters!

Doing what really matters has both professional and personal significance for me. I always try to approach life with a mindset for growth, though I must admit that I recently had a most challenging year.

I began the summer battling a rash on my face that was accompanied by extremely high fevers. After numerous visits to my primary doctor, the dermatologist, the medical specialist, and the hospital, it was finally determined that I am highly allergic to a medication that I must take. After an adjustment to my medication, it took three months for my face to return to normal. Next, my mom's health continued to decline and after several new health concerns arose, I made the heart-wrenching decision to move her in to an assisted-living home. She is adjusting well but it was a very difficult first few months. In the spring, my future mother-in-law died after battling a painful, degenerative disease. It is especially hard to watch someone you love grieving the loss of their mother.

My professional life was equally challenging. There were tense contract negotiations with the union, sensitive and controversial student discipline issues, a failed budget, and a school year that ended with the loss of two elementary students, which had a significant impact on the entire community.

Emotionally, intellectually, and physically I was drained. I needed a moment to regroup and recharge so I decided to take my mom to Washington, D.C. for a long weekend. One of our stops involved going to the MLK Memorial. Although I've been to D.C. many times, this visit to the memorial was a first for me. As I silently walked up to the building I stared in awe at the image of a man who typifies the phrase; *Do what matters*. Then, as I strolled the promenade, I read each additional MLK quote, stopping at one that reads: *The ultimate measure of a man is not where he stands in moments of comfort and convenience, but where he stands during times of challenge and controversy.*

It was at that moment that my entire year came into view and I realized that it wasn't about being comfortable or convenient but rather about staying the course, connecting with others, and ensuring I participated in doing what matters.

What is the leadership lesson relative to doing what matters? We live in a society where the little things we do are often overlooked, which has a way of making us believe those things don't matter. They absolutely do! Empathy, understanding, kindness, and a willingness to reach out to others matters.

I've also learned that transparency and vulnerability are important too. Some of the deepest relationships I have started with being open and honest and comfortable enough to show the real Lesli Clara Myers. So today and always, remember that kindness, appreciation, thoughtfulness, acknowledgement, and openness may seem small but are truly the things that matter.

Are you making time to do those things that matter to you and those around you?

Selah...

Dr. L

Reflection / Action Items

_____
_____
_____
_____
_____
_____
_____
_____
_____
_____
_____
_____
_____
_____
_____
_____
_____
_____
_____
_____

LCM Leadership Lesson #30
Finding common ground.

Almost forty years ago I experienced a wonderfully magical moment; that of meeting my best friend. I hopped on the school bus where our eyes immediately met. She was sitting alone in her seat looking frightened and sad. I walked up to her and asked if she wanted to be friends to which she promptly said, "Yes!" That single interaction was the beginning of an instant kinship.

She and I were inseparable. We lived within seven houses of each other and saw each other every day. We studied together, played together, and quickly became a part of each other's families. Her father was a devout Hindu from India. I was fascinated by her family traditions and learned much about Indian culture. Each week, I tried new and exciting dishes that smelled and tasted wonderful. To this day, Indian food is one of my favorites.

My *bestie* in turn became knowledgeable of African-American culture and was especially fascinated with the house of worship I attended. I grew up in the Pentecostal church and she was amazed at how long service lasted on Sundays and that we attended church on other evenings as well for prayer meetings and bible study.

Our friendship blossomed over the years and although she left right after high school to attend the University of California, Berkeley, we've stayed in touch. We celebrated various milestones throughout the years and I was honored to be the only non-family member to participate in her extremely sacred wedding ceremony.

My friend recently came to visit me though we had not physically seen each other in over 20 years. We reminisced about old times. We noted the very many rich things that made us different (our cultures, our backgrounds, our families), and we celebrated them. What we had previously failed to note and acknowledge however, were our commonalities.

We both loved tennis, and we wore clothing from second hand shops, though we never talked about it because of peer pressure related to wearing just the right thing. And because of shame and embarrassment, we never knew that our mothers were dealing with similar challenges at home.

When we suddenly recognized we could have held each other up through some very difficult times, we cried over the fact that we had missed out on opportunities to further deepen our relationship.

So, what makes this leadership lesson important? Though it is imperative and helpful to look for opportunities in fostering diversity, it is equally important to find shared commonalities.

How do you personally and professionally find common ground with those you are associated with?

Selah...

Dr. L

Personal Reflection / Action Items

_____

_____

_____

_____

_____

_____

_____

_____

_____

_____

_____

_____

_____

_____

_____

_____

_____

_____

_____

_____

_____

_____

_____

_____

LCM Leadership Lesson #31
Think on these three things.

My maternal grandmother (aka Nana) was a
formidable woman. She married around the age of 13,
had 10 children, and was widowed before the age of 29.
She stood 5'10" and had piercing hazel brown eyes. I
loved to sit with Nana and hear about her life growing
up in the south. I especially enjoyed when that gleam
in her eye would appear signifying one of her infamous
stories was about to begin.

About four months before my Nana died, she called me
over to sit with her. It was August, I was eleven, and
we were in town for a family gathering. She told me
that she wouldn't always be around and that she had
an important story to share with me. I got into *story
listening position* as she unfolded what would be her
final *leadership lesson* to me.

She said, "There are three pieces of advice I'd like to
share with you: 1). Always ensure you maintain your
faith and belief in God because with Him, all things are
possible. 2). Continually pursue education and get as
much of it as you can. Money, fame, and fortune can be
stripped away from you, but once you obtain knowledge
through education, it's yours to keep." At this point in
the story, Nana leaned forward, in the way that only
she could, to offer one final piece of advice, purposely
pausing for effect. "Nana, what is the last piece of
advice? Please tell me, please!" "And finally, 3). Stay
away from nasty tail boys because they are nothing but

trouble!" As I laughed, my grandmother hugged me and told me how proud she was of me and how excited she was for what was to come.

Her advice easily translates into leadership lessons. Keep the faith and be hopeful, pursue educational and professional development opportunities, and choose your closest relationships wisely. My Nana's stories continue to ring in my mind. I miss her and am so grateful for the precious time I had with her. I owe many of my personal and professional accomplishments to her. Now, it's my responsibility to continue the storytelling tradition...

What core values guide you? Who and where did they come from? To whom might you pass them on?

Selah...

Dr. L

Reflection/Action Items

_____

_____

_____

_____

_____

_____

_____

_____

_____

_____

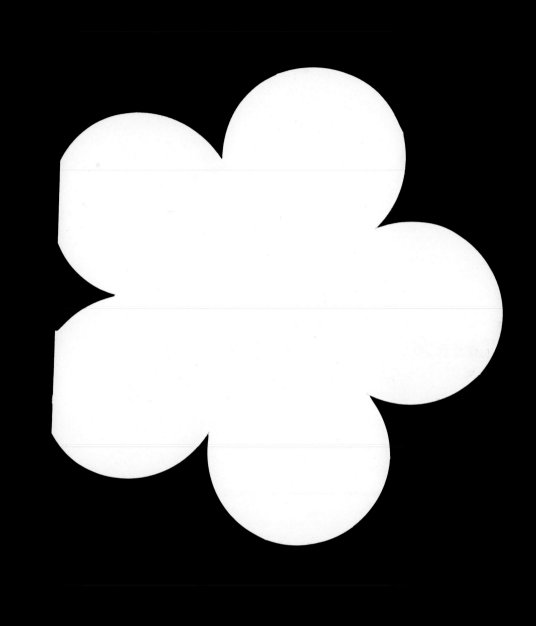

About the Author

Brockport Central School District Superintendent Dr. Lesli C. Myers has dedicated her life to the pursuit of high quality education. She is the first African-American woman to become Superintendent of Schools in Monroe County and has served Brockport Central School District in that role since 2012.

Dr. Myers received her bachelor's degree in Psychology and a master's degree in Counseling and Human Development from the University of Rochester. She also earned a master's degree in Urban Educational Administration and her Doctorate of Education in Executive Leadership from Saint John Fisher College.

Throughout her career, Dr. Myers has had a tremendous impact on the field of education. She is the first African-American president of the New York State School Counselor Association. She appeared before the United States Congress and her testimony, in part, resulted in a spending bill that included the largest increase (77.5 percent) ever to the Elementary and Secondary School Counseling Program.

Dr. Myers has received many prestigious honors that reflect her dedication to education and community, including the BreakThru Magazine Empowering Award, NYS Women of Distinction Award, Rochester Business Journal *40 Under 40*, Saint John Fisher Distinguished Alumni Award, Urban League of

Rochester Educator Award, and Western New York School Counselors Consortium Lifetime Achievement Award. Additionally, she was named a 2016 Athena Award finalist.

Dr. Myers has designed and conducted workshops and presentations for elementary and secondary students, undergraduate and graduate students, varied educators, and many others at the local, regional, and national level.

She presented, *Racism: A Mere Pigment of the Imagination*, at the 2017 TEDx ROCHESTER event. Her style is humorous, straightforward, and sincere, and she encourages people of all ages and backgrounds to creatively use their abilities and talents to serve others.

Dr. Myers is passionate about her professional work and volunteerism, and looks forward to many years of continued service to students, parents, teachers, and administrators.

Made in the USA
Monee, IL
02 September 2021